D1123293

Stepping-Stones:
A Garden Path

Stepping-Stones:
A Garden Path

Patsy Clairmont

VINE
BOOKS

SERVANT PUBLICATIONS
ANN ARBOR, MICHIGAN

©2001 by Patsy Clairmont
All rights reserved.

Vine Books is an imprint of Servant Publications especially designed to serve evangelical Christians.

Unless otherwise noted, Scripture quotations are from The Holy Bible, New International Version (NIV) ©1973, 1984 by International Bible Society, used by permission of Zondervan Publishing House.

"Bird Brain" is from *God Uses Cracked Pots* by Patsy Clairmont, a Focus on the Family book published by Tyndale House Publishers. ©1991 by Patsy Clairmont. All rights reserved. International copyright secured. Used by permission.

"Bouquet" is from *Normal Is Just a Setting on Your Dryer* by Patsy Clairmont, a Focus on the Family book published by Tyndale House Publishers. ©1993 by Patsy Clairmont. All rights reserved. International copyright secured. Used by permission.

The personal contributions of friends to this book have been included by permission.

Published by Servant Publications
P. O. Box 8617
Ann Arbor, Michigan 48107

Editor: Janet Kobobel Grant
Photography: Bob Foran. Additional photography by Patsy Clairmont, Danya Clairmont, and Diane Bareis.
Cover design: Alan Furst

01 02 03 04 10 9 8 7 6 5 4 3 2 1
Printed in the United States of America
ISBN 1-56955-150-2

Dedication

**To Janet Kobobel Grant,
who is shade to my soul.**

Contents

Acknowledgments / 9

Introduction:

How Does Your Garden Grow? / 11

Stepping Through Spring

A Garden Path / 16

Stepping-Stones / 18

Open House / 21

Garden Parables / 23

Honeybunches / 25

More Bees, Please / 27

Bzzz … / 28

Bouquet … / 30

Gardens are … / 33

Desert Eden / 34

Gardening Tips I / 35

Not Those Nuts Again! / 37

The Invitation / 39

Stepping Through Summer

Dawn Delights / 43

Summer Choruses / 44

Bobbing in the Breezes / 47

Kneelers / 49

Wild, Weed-Whacking Woman / 54

A-Shedding We Shall Go / 57

Lost Path / 61

Gardening Tips II / 63

Bird Brain / 65

Garden Patch / 69

Garden Hymn / 72

Stepping Through Autumn

Autumn Ambiance / 77

Stone Garden / 80

Poetry in a Vine / 83

Garden Glossary / 85

A Parade of Roses:

A Trilogy of Love Stories

Love's Bloom / 86

A Profusion of Petals / 88

The Wedding Gift / 90

Garden Artist / 93

Gardening Tips III / 96

Fall's Fireworks / 98

Stepping Through Winter

The Winter Ball / 104

You Can't Do That / 107

Winter's Grip / 109

Deck the Halls / 111

Hummers / 114

Gardening Tips IV / 116

Bouquet Blues / 117

Winter Tree / 121

For Every Season

All Things He Does Well / 122

Acknowledgments

*J*ust as a garden takes more than good fortune to come to fruition, so with a book. Many folks were instrumental in the growth of *Stepping-Stones*.

Servant Publications once again lived up to its servant image by offering support in many tangible ways—from final edit work (Kathryn Deering), to design, to—get this—hands-on, down-in-the-dirt help with planting. Now that's impressive. Thanks to Don Cooper and Bert Ghezzi for this opportunity to grow a good book. A big hurrah to Diane Bareis, art director, for her tireless efforts and her gentle expertise.

Thanks to Bob Foran, the photographer, who understands the importance of a clear focus. His gifted lens-angles and his sweet disposition make him a joy to work with.

Thanks to Todd's Landscaping Services (especially Mike) and Botanicals by Design for their efforts to make our land blossom with vibrancy and style.

When Rick Pherson constructed my garden shed, I was like a child with her first lollipop. Rick listened to the dream in my mind and then built it into existence. Thank you.

Kudos to Janet Grant for adding so many seeds to this manuscript. Your creativity, passion, and editing prowess are a gift to my life.

A special thanks to my nephew Steve McEuen for his quotations. Kisses and hugs to Jim and Erin Oliver for the photos of their daughters, Riley and Rachel.

Thanks to my children Jason, Danya, Marty, and my darling husband of thirty-eight years, Les. In the life of a garden, you, dear man, are my sturdy, steady oak.

Since writing this book I have become a grandma to an adorable grandson, Justin. What a generational blessing. May we remember that the gardens we seed today will help insure a luxuriant land filled with life and lessons for future generations. Plant wisely.

Gardens can be a family effort.
(From front to back: daughter-in-law, Dany...
Patsy; son, Jason; husband, Les.)

How Does Your Garden Grow?

Mary, Mary, quite contrary, how does your garden grow?"

Actually, that's a great question, and impressed passersby who want to have "the touch" often ask gardeners just that. Some gardeners truly are gifted with a green thumb, but others are just plain gutsy, and at best their digits are streaky shades of chartreuse.

That, folks, would be me. Yup, streaky Patsy. I, like Mary, actually know more about growing a good case of contrary than I do a patch of carnations. Although one summer I did find a small swath of miniature carnations that survived my tampering. Their pretty little frilly-fringed faces graced tiny vases throughout my home that year.

Gardens for me are more about romance than, say, rakes. Have you read the Song of Songs lately? Note how the lovers linger in the garden and gather lilies and spices. Oh, heart be still!

Of course, without a stout rake, romance would quickly be buried under the debris off the nearest maple. But I can honestly say I don't wake up spouting joy over the thought of having a brisk raking session. I do, however, enter a day sprightlier when I can saunter through petaled paths gathering an armload of (sigh) lilies as I go.

Not only do I love the romance of a garden, I also appreciate its artistic wonder. Which did our heavenly Gardener do first: sculpt a rose, watercolor a hydrangea, or tint the morning glories the color of the sky?

When you visit an art museum, have you noticed how room after room abounds with renderings of gardens—more specifically of flowers? We're smitten with floral beauty, all the way from a giant sunflower down to a wee violet.

So taken are we that we try in our own ways to reproduce the look of nature in our art and in our homes. I personally love bringing flowers indoors (more about that later) so I can linger in the fragrance and marvel in the intricacies of their designs.

Many people will tell you they find gardening medicinal, and I would have to agree, although these days, I find that once I get down near the earth, getting back up has become an acrobatic feat. And by the time I've weeded several beds, deadheaded the petunias, repotted the hostas, planted bulbs, and watered the thirsty rhododendrons, I'm ready for a therapeutic massage. No wonder Mary was so contrary! Yet all those aches and pains seem a small price when one steps out the door to behold the lush results, hearing the *oohs* and *aahs* of others as they ask the all-important question, "How does your garden grow?"

Stepping-Stones celebrates the garden and invites us to follow the garden path together, taking delight in the sights, sounds, and fragrances that thrill our senses. We'll listen to the birds warble and trill, we'll pause to photograph a moment worth capturing, we'll design an arrangement, we'll fuss with our tools, we'll play in our garden shed, we'll squeal with wonder at new sprouts and blossoms. And we'll walk and talk with the One who created the first Garden that we might know the pleasure of His company.

Stepping Through
SPRING

Spring's melody causes hearts to rejoice.
A resurrection hymn … let's lift our voice!

A Garden Path

In Michigan, spring is as elusive as a butterfly with hiccups. Between snowflakes, spring pops up in the form of white-petaled snowdrops or as a purple crocus. Then the season disappears again under a fresh, six-inch snowfall, only to reemerge some sunny day as a grape hyacinth. This hide-and-seek game keeps us Michiganders from being disheartened despite the fact that our snow shovels remain on full alert. We know that soon our landscape will make a dramatic turn as spring overtakes winter and lays full claim to the land.

What's your favorite spring flower? Naming a single favorite is difficult because the lineup is so show-stopping gorgeous. Who, for instance, can scurry past a lilac bush in bloom? Why, the fragrance causes even grown men to stop in their tracks, breathe deeply, and reminisce. With one whiff suddenly we're kids again, racing our bikes past bushes heavy with purple and white displays.

Tulips are the seasonal flags that tout spring's victory over winter's barrenness. I love to see their lovely, silken heads swaying in the breeze. Tulips' sturdy stems and vibrant colors decorate the landscape with beauty. Few things are more beautiful than a bouquet of white tulips in a clear vase.

Spring's lilies of the valley often are found clustered together in shady patches under the protection of a bush or a tree, where they tend to flourish. As a child it seemed to me that, if one were ever to catch a glimpse of a thimble-sized fairy, it would be under the tiny white bells of this dainty plant. I'm almost certain that garden fairies are the only ones privy to hear the gentle chimes of this whimsical harbinger of spring's fragrant season.

At times in my life I've been emotionally buried under a wintry blast of problems, wondering if I would ever experience spring's transformation. Once in a while I would feel hopeful at signs of change, but then the biting winds of adversity would engulf me again. I've lived long enough now that I've learned, just as surely as spring eventually gains on winter, our hardships lessen, and we will make it through. I'm grateful to the One who offers to accompany us each step of the way, regardless of the season or intensity of the storm.

Stepping-Stones

I'm a fiddler, not as in Stradivarius but as in flower-fiddling. I like to photograph them, gather them, arrange them, and admire them. I even enjoy weeding—especially once it's done.

One sunny day not long after moving into our current house, I felt the urge to fiddle in a perennial flowerbed in the front yard. As I rambled about the garden, I stopped from time to time to examine a flower or to watch a butterfly zigzag across the yard. At

one point I knelt down to weed a small patch of Johnny-jump-ups that had lived up to their name, catapulting themselves up through thick layers of wood chips.

As I weeded around the colorful flowers, something that looked like a rock caught my eye amidst the chips. I reached for the object, thinking I would pull up a pebble. Instead I uncovered a small stepping-stone. With growing curiosity I scouted around and found another stone buried beneath layers of the wood chips one step from the last one. Feeling I was on a mission, I moved over a bit, and yes, discovered another stone. Soon I had uncovered seven of them. Guess where they led? To the water spigot.

I found that small incident typifies what happens often in my life. I'll feel uncertain about the next step I should take. I'll look around at the somewhat—OK, OK—the *very* weedy landscape of my life, and I won't see any obvious path. Then something will happen. Maybe I'll amble onto a Scripture that exposes a hidden step, or my path will zigzag across someone else's and that person will point me in the correct direction, or my weedy circumstances will cause me to kneel in His presence and from that position I'll see what I had missed before.

Let's not fiddle around and miss the stepping-stones that lead to His provision, His living water, the spigot that never runs dry.

Open House

After enduring a long winter, I feel twinges of joy when I spot, atop a fencepost, my first robin casing out the snow-spotted landscape.

Robins are seldom wrong, you know, about spring's approach. Oh, overly optimistic perhaps, but never wrong. And if you find a purple crocus peeking through a snowdrift *and* spot a robin in the same day, well, break out the swimsuit, honey, the pool is about to open. OK, OK, maybe not the pool, but perhaps the potting shed.

Opening my potting shed is more fun than the opening of a new mall (and I love to shop). When I open the shed, I don't have to leave home, search for a parking place, or max out my credit card. Instead, I dust off the tools, arrange my packets of seeds or seedlings, and make sketches and lists of what I want to do.... Uh-oh, we may need to visit the mall (nursery), after all.

I love the view from my potting shed. It overlooks my back-yard flowerbeds. From the shed I can follow the pattern of the crisscrossing stepping-stones as they curve and wind from one bed to another, from my back door all the way to the shed's door. At one point the path slips through the iron trellis that serves as the entry into my gardens.

I enjoy watching garden guests appear and make their way to me in the shed, where the top of the Dutch door stands ajar, awaiting their arrival. I sit perched in front of the window, where I try my best to look horticultural (a few quick smudges of soil strategically placed on the forehead and lower arm can be convincing). My potting shed is built of cedar, which makes the visit inside fragrant in a woodsy way (if you like cedar—and obviously I do).

Throughout the spring, summer, and autumn some of my visitors fly into the shed. They never knock. The most distracting ones buzz. But bees aren't as annoying when they circle your head as the falsetto-pitched mosquitoes. Those little singing terrorists are out for blood. Early in the season I have to dust webs the size of New Hampshire, and sweep out the spiders, itsy-bitsy and otherwise, plus a few good luck ladybugs.

Even when unexpected guests (like a garden snake) show up, I must say the view from the potting shed is worth the risk. For from there I'm the queen of the peonies, daisies, hostas, and weeds. I'm the temporary proprietor of the daylilies, lilacs, wiegelia, and sedum. I'm the hostess for the robins, rabbits, raccoons, and wrens. And I am the grateful recipient, observer, and appreciator of the wonders of God's creation.

Garden Parables

Creator God began human life in Eden. Eden was not on a mountaintop, not in a cavern, not twenty leagues under the sea, but in a lush garden. I like that.

I believe God's signature is all over the earth, but especially in our little Edens. He has amended the soil with life-lessons, and the produce (flowers, fruits, vegetables) is meant to nurture us with truth and beauty and cause us to see Him in all things.

Take, for instance, the seed. What a miracle! Get this, it has no brain, and yet it knows exactly what it will be when it grows up. (I'm still trying to figure that one out.) We never see a morning glory seed strain to produce tomatoes, nor have I caught my pansies huffing and puffing in an attempt to grow into svelte lilies. Instead, this diminutive encasement follows its Creator's plan and purpose right down to the blossom.

Have you ever considered that the seed is like a blueprint in that it contains all the information to produce not only a stem, but also leaves, blossoms, stamen, sepals, and pistil? How did that much potential ever get stuffed inside something so tiny?

And another thing about this amazing nugget is that it's willing to do all its work out of the limelight, underground, and to allow the stalks and blooms to receive the applause. We never hear anyone say, "Wow, that was one grand effort by that seed to produce such beauty. Hooray, seed!" Instead we hear, "Oh, look at that flower, isn't it spectacular?"

Yes, the garden flourishes with parables, from the seed that dies to give life, the single stem that pushes its way through concrete, the tree that is damaged in the storm and grows more beautiful after the trauma.

Patrick, beekeeper extraordinaire, is abuzz about his business.

Honeybunches

*H*oney, come here!" The excitement in my husband's voice caused me to abandon my computer and sprint through our California condo to our back bedroom. Les was standing next to the door, pointing out onto our walled patio.

I looked for a moment before I figured out what I was seeing. At first it appeared to be a thick cloud spinning around, but on second glance I realized that the cloud was *bees*. Hundreds and hundreds and hundreds of bees. I thought we were in a Hitchcock movie.

I called the office of our complex to alert them to the invasion and to get help. They called a bee specialist, who buzzed over to our place. By the time he arrived, the cloud of buzzers had formed a foot-and-a-half-long dangling cluster off a branch in our ficus tree. The elongated clump of moving bee bodies looked like dark grapes, except these were humming Jimmy Rogers' rendition of "Honeycomb."

Later I was informed that the queen bee was in the cluster's center, and the others surrounded her to protect her. I also learned that they were looking for a place to live and had decided to hang out in our tree until a decision was made about their new abode.

The beekeeper, Patrick, was an amiable young fellow with a purple bee tattooed on his neck (ouch). He said these were honeybees. Whew! I had feared that the killer bees we had heard about on TV newscasts were about to make us a 6 o'clock featured item.

Patrick donned his minimal gear, a safari helmet draped in netting, climbed a ladder, and vacuumed up our little darlings. All thirty-six thousand of them. Yep, Patrick estimated our hive contained thirty-six thousand bees, which, on the numerical scale, comes just before a gazillion.

Our beekeeper brought a male bee to the door to show me that they don't have stingers. As I pressed my nose against the glass to get a good view, I was a tad dismayed to learn that it's the *girls* who leave stinging memories, which they did to poor Patrick while he was educating me. He had grabbed Don Juan for the show-and-tell, and some of D.J.'s lady friends decided to teach Patrick a lesson. It seemed effective. Patrick dropped Donnie Boy and headed to his truck until the girls settled down.

After slurping up the hive with his shop vac, Patrick told us that, when the bees settled down, he would release them into a hive. He had forty-one hives ... now forty-two.

Patrick said beekeeping is a honey-filled life, but I think I'll stick to writing, in which the only sting is my editor's corrections (just kidding, sweet Janet).

More Bees, Please

*M*y friend Thelma Wells is in a buzz over bees and what they represent. In fact, she wears a bee every day—yes, every day. She says they are a God-designed reminder that we can overcome life's obstacles. You see, Thelma knows that bumblebees shouldn't be able to fly because their bodies are too heavy and their wingspan too shallow. Yet … bzzz.

There are many kinds of bees, including cellophane bees, mining bees, sweat bees, leaf-cutting bees, cuckoo bees (honest), mason bees, digger bees, and the most common, the bumblebee's cousin, honeybees.

Honeybees are the sweetest for obvious reasons, and they do gardeners a great service. The worker bees load up the tiny hairs that cover their bodies with pollen from a flower's center and carry that pollen back to their hives, where the pollen is used to feed their young (larvae). While buzzing from one blossom to another, bees cross-pollinate our flowers, which is extremely important if they are to continue to bloom. Bees also harvest nectar that is carried to the hives and transformed into honey, nature's sweetest produce. Honey is mentioned in Scripture to represent sweetness (of course) but also to symbolize pleasure and delight.

And, honey, nothing is sweeter than slathering that stuff over a homemade baking powder biscuit dripping in butter. A hot cup of peppermint tea yummied up with a teaspoon of honey is a wonderful thing. Some say that even allergies (ah-ah-choo!) are helped if one will eat local honey, which acts as an antidote for area blossoms.

In some ways we are like bees that have the potential to bring sweetness or to leave a stinging reminder of our presence. Of course, only the female honeybees have stingers…. Phooey, that's more applicable than I want to ponder. Let's just agree with Thelma and move on: Three cheers for the bee!

B_{ZZZ}...

Did you know ...

... That bees have taken the term "frequent flyer" to the heights, as they travel fifty-five thousand miles to produce one pound of honey? Yikes! I wonder if they ever upgrade to first class?

... That to manufacture one pound of honey, those sweethearts must visit—get this—two million flowers? Zowie!

... That Utah is known as the Beehive State? What a bunch of honeys.

... That bees dance? I'm not sure if it's the boogie-woogie or the Charleston, but the arriving bee's circular dance tells the awaiting bees where the bee has been. Then the other bees repeat the dance steps and follow the pattern to find the flowers.

... That only one queen lives in each hive? Figures. When a new queen is born, one of them has to leave, and a break-off colony follows the departing queen to assist in forming a new hive. Long live queenie!

... That the average U.S. citizen consumes one pound of honey a year? Hmm, I put that much in a pot of chamomile tea. But then, I've never been accused of being average (or normal).

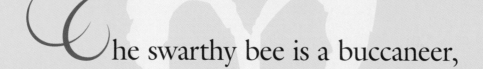

The swarthy bee is a buccaneer,

A burly velveted rover,

Who loves the booming wind in his ear

As he sails the seas of clover.

Bliss Carman,
"A More Ancient Mariner"

Bouquet

I am a woman who loves receiving presents. Fortunately, I'm married to a man who gets a kick out of buying me surprises.

He also is famous, in a spontaneous moment, for whisking me off to a mall to shop for a new outfit. It's not unusual for us to go into a dress shop and have Les want to buy more for me than I would for myself. That causes quite a reaction from the sales clerks, since his attitude isn't the norm. They all want to know how I trained Les to be that way. Unfortunately, I can't take credit. (I love credit, too.) He just has that kind of giving heart.

I remember our nineteenth wedding anniversary, when Les wrote me a little poem that I still cherish.

Roses are red, violets are blue,

If I had it to do over again,

I'd still marry you!

The poem was especially dear to me because Les and I married when we were seventeen and eighteen, and we had been through some challenging years (financially, physically, and emotionally), including my period of agoraphobia. From time to time, I had wondered if he regretted his choice. So even though the poem didn't exactly start off originally, it ended for me like a masterpiece.

Over the years (thirty), Les has given me gifts that have made me laugh, cry, gasp, and even learn some lessons. One sunny spring day, Les came bounding into the house clutching two apricot sweetheart rosebuds for me. I, of course, was delighted.

The flowers came with a powdered mix to lengthen their blooming time; I stirred it into the water. I gave each rose a fresh cut and then slipped them into one of the many vases Les had given me in his years of continual courting. I set my mini-bouquet in the living room, being careful to protect it from direct sun and yet giving it visibility for my enjoyment.

As the days went by, I was fascinated by what happened. My seemingly identical roses responded very differently to their environment. One began to open slowly, and at each stage of development, she was exquisite. Her unfolding presentation pleased me and added beauty and wonder to the room. Finally, my apricot beauty dropped her petals in a breathtaking farewell performance.

In contrast, the other rose seemed stuck in her beginning. She held tenaciously to her baby form. In the end, the brooding bud turned brown and hung over the edge of the vase like a tragic teardrop.

For days I thought about the contrast. I've always applauded rosebuds as romantic. Yet it seemed sad and unnatural to see a flower begin and end at the same place. The bud that didn't open never reached her potential. She never released the sweet fragrance placed within her to share with others. Her death portrayed regret and sadness.

I could celebrate even the loss of the open rose, knowing she had accomplished all she was designed to do. Her fragrance lingered in our home even after the vase was removed.

My friend Vella was a flower in the fullest sense. When she was told she had only a short time to live and that her cancer was the most painful of cancers, instead of closing up, she spread her petals all the way open and bathed us in the fragrance of faith. We wouldn't have blamed her if she had drawn into a bud and died privately in her pain. But Vella saw this illness as her farewell performance, an opportunity for as long as she had left to fulfill the design God had for her. Vella lived out her remaining days with exquisite grace. Dropping her last petal, her parting words were, "Praise the Lord." Then she fell asleep and was gone.

Family and friends could celebrate her life and her homegoing. At the time of this writing, it has been eleven years since she left us . . . and her fragrance still lingers. Because there's a great deal of cancer in my family, I sometimes wonder how I would handle it if I were to be diagnosed with the dreaded disease. I'm not a brave person … except in my imagination. There I'm valiant, noble, and steadfast. In reality, I whine when I get a cold.

Three years ago, I watched my dear, seventy-three-year-old mother endure surgery for breast cancer. She went through her diagnosis, surgery, and radiation not only with courage but also with sweetness and humor. That gave me hope.

I want, whatever my environment, to be growing and fragrant; I don't want to be closed and unable to open up to others emotionally. I don't want to die holding to myself what I should have given away.

Les' gift of roses, pressed between the pages of my memory, has been a poignant reminder: Openness is a risk, growth is its reward, and His grace makes it all possible.

Gardens are ...

- *A pleasure.* What a visual reprieve from pavement, traffic, and crowds.

- *A tranquil place for contemplation.* My brain cells think better encircled by lilacs, lilies, and lavender.

- *A perfect "room" for entertaining.* Who doesn't love a garden?

- *A constant supplement to our understanding of who God is* and how He continues to work in our lives (cultivating, pruning, and harvesting).

- *A gentle way to add beauty and life* to a tainted planet marred by crime, hostility, and heartbreak.

- *A healing environment for bruised emotions.*

- *A harvest of joy.* Embrace an armload of peonies for a fresh sense of God's handiwork.

- *A place to pray.* Even Jesus thought so.

Desert Eden

The first time I flew into a desert area, I gazed, fascinated and bewildered, out the airplane window. "Where's the green?" I asked Les. "Where are the trees?"

"Patsy, it's the desert—as in sand, cacti, and—*beep-beep*—roadrunners."

"Yes, but …" I trailed off as I continued to stare at the soft beige land stretching endlessly out below me. I knew deserts weren't grass-covered, yet I was still stunned by its barrenness.

By the end of my desert stay, I had learned to love the elegant palm trees, the soft-sculpted sands, and even the rolling tumbleweeds that typify the arid climate. Initially, though, I found it disconcerting compared to the lush greenery of my home state.

But since then I've learned the desert has its share of show-stopping flowers that emerge sporadically from dry drifts of sand. Two years ago during a desert stay, the rains came with such surprising frequency that the sands burst forth in an abundant, vivid yellow and festive purple carpet. People who had lived in the desert for twenty years had never seen such color.

I thought, *Imagine that, all those seeds and flowers have been asleep, hidden in the sands, waiting to burst forth with beauty and color.*

Wow! Makes one wonder what seeds of greatness lie just below our surface. Perhaps we shouldn't be so quick to pop open our umbrellas at the first sign of a storm, but instead should invite the rain to water our parched souls. Then perhaps we, too, will be like Zion: "He [the Lord] will make her deserts like Eden, her wastelands like the garden of the Lord" (Isaiah 51:3b).

gardening tips I

Ginny, Southern California

"I've always enjoyed gardening, but two years ago I decided to plant an English garden. With a knowledgeable friend's help, I developed a plan.

"I spent several weeks preparing the soil, planting each bush and flower, and tending to every new little growth. I had no idea—nor did my family—how much work this would involve! But we were rewarded in the spring when my whole garden, even in its first bloom, was an abundant expanse of color and beauty. Every time I walked outside, it brought joy to my heart.

"Along the way, I've learned a few tips:

1. I used some wonderful linking fences that are made from green metal poles, much like a simple stake, but bent at the top in a right angle, about four inches long. At the end of this angle is a loop, which can be linked to the next pole. You can link as many of these together as necessary, depending on the size of the shrub you want to support. They keep branches from falling on the ground and keep your plant's stems from breaking when

the weight becomes too heavy. The poles come in different heights, are straight or curved, and are especially nice for leggy plants like penstemon.

2. I love working with window boxes, but one challenge is keeping the dirt well drained. To correct this, make sure the wooden box has adequate holes for drainage. If you use a plastic liner, that also must have holes. Because window boxes are by nature small and narrow, removing and replanting only one flower is difficult. I've solved both problems. First, instead of putting the soil in the box, use four-inch potted plants or three- to six-packs of small plants. Then you can take the plants out of the box to water them and allow them to drain. Replacing flowers as they grow is also simplified. Now my window boxes look healthy and fresh.

3. Be creative! Don't just try the common varieties of plants you're familiar with. Experiment with various bulbs, too. The blooms you get will surprise and amaze you."

Not Those Nuts Again!

I had longed for a spring crop of flowers at our new home, but my autumn was crowded with speaking engagements. I figured if I didn't hire outside help, I wouldn't achieve my goal. So I engaged an enterprising couple from my community to do a fall bulb planting on my behalf. One chilly day the wife and a couple of young workers showed up and planted around two hundred bulbs (ah, aerobic youth). I was elated.

Winter blew in not long after the planting and hung around like unemployed relatives. Les and I decided to scamper west to dodge some of the icy wind and snowy walkways, and by the time we returned, spring had come. Tulips, hyacinths, and daffodils greeted us with just the cheery welcome we were hoping for.

As I surveyed our groupings of flowers, I noticed a small flock of red tulips huddled against the fence. Hmm, now how did they get way over there? I walked toward the fence for a closer look. The scarlet flowers were at least twenty feet away from where they had been planted.

The next day my neighbor leaned over the fence and called

out, "Thank you." Unsure of what I had done, I joined him at the fence. "Thank you? What did I do?"

"Thanks for the tulips."

"I gave you tulips?"

"Sort of," he replied. "A squirrel dug up your bulbs and replanted them throughout the neighbor-hood. Quite the horticulturist, the little fellow traveled from yard to yard, distributing the wealth. The neighbor behind you was delighted to find a flourishing mound of yellow and red tulips near his garage."

Oh, great. Just my luck to have a nutty squirrel with a Johnny Appleseed complex. What a little thief!

Do you have any marauders in your life? Scripture tells us that "the little foxes … ruin the vineyards" (Song of Songs 2:15). I find little attitude "foxes" color my disposition, little words separate friends, and little irritations light my fuse.

A little can go a long way. On the positive side, a little effort can complete a half-done task, a little time can improve a seemingly hopeless situation, a little thoughtfulness can help mend a broken heart, and a little faith—hey, watch out—can move mountains.

The Invitation

Join me in the lilacs,
Meet me by the tree.
We'll tip our teacups
Until half-past three.

Wear your straw-ribboned hat,
Your white satin gloves.
We'll sing to the birds,
Teach hymns to the doves.

We'll speak of the weather,
The blossoms and bees,
Immerse dainty scones
Into soft whipped cheese.

We'll whisper sweet secrets
That nest in our minds
Then giggle and weep,
Reliving dear times.

Stepping Through
SUMMER

*S*ummer brings a gentler pace
Tatting fields in Queen Anne's lace.

Dawn Delights

*A*h, the early hours of a summer garden, when the flowers are drenched in dew. I love to see the diamond droplets that sparkle in the first sun rays and to eavesdrop on the sparrows' exhilarating morning praise, soprano-clear. Sounds are crisper and time is less relevant as nature carefully unfolds her lovely trousseau.

Something is sacred about meandering down my stepping-stone path in those sweet, dayspring moments. Sunlight dapples the stones and edges the daylilies and dahlias in amber warmth. The winding path leads beyond the lavender hostas, pink foxgloves, and deep purple salvia. At one point I pass a pair of Adirondack chairs and then reconsider the decision to walk on, knowing these maiden moments of the day will soon be over. I ease down into the slanted wood and find it a perfect fit. Leaning back, I allow myself to be enveloped in dawn's elixir.

Then into the sublime trickles the ridiculous: real life. The increase of traffic sounds slowly begins to rattle uninvited into the garden intermingled with neighbors' voices calling necessary instructions to one another. Train whistles whine warnings in the distance, and my husband's loving inquiry drifts over the lilacs, "Honey, where are you?"

"Hiding in the early light," I answer. "Will you join me?"

He does, and the sunrise finale becomes even sweeter shared.

Summer Choruses

I am neither right-brained nor left-brained. Yep, you guessed it: I'm bird-brained. I love our feathered friends' flight patterns, warbles, and visits. Often a robin or blue jay will sit atop my trellis to rest a spell from its busy day. The robins are especially delighted with fresh-turned soil in my flowerbeds; it makes the extraction of din-din so much easier. In return the robins fill my yard with song. I reckon it's their version of singing for their supper.

A robin's rhapsody is one thing, but the choir director needs to have a chat with the blue jays. Blue jays don't sing, they squawk. Even though they are terrorists at heart, jays make handsome statements in their dapper suits. And when they aren't hoodwinking smaller birds, their distinctive shrill sends chills up the spines of every frog within a three-mile radius. Blue jays are related to crows, ravens, and magpies, and unfortunately they have a notorious habit of pilfering other birds' nests. Boo!

We have ducks that occasionally drop (and I do mean "drop") by, who are true comediennes. They quack me up.

Tiny goldfinches zip into my garden like streaks of butter to repose on tall cone flowers, and then, as quickly as they arrive, they dart off. These lively yellow birds seem pleased that my neighbor's blue spruce trees have spread their branches, in the friendliest way, through our adjoining fence. I see the goldfinches' bright yellow suits with their black and white trim flash from limb to limb as they flutter about.

Another aerobic bird, and one of my personal favorites, is the black-capped chickadee, which often can be seen dangling upside down off a pinecone or twittering atop a fence post. He, too, finds refuge in the huge spruce branches and dashes about my garden whistling while he works. There's nothing like a good whistle to improve the environment, and often the melodious sound will lead into some rousing chorus to which even bystanders join in.

Chickadees are quite relational and out of friendly curiosity will even perch on one's finger. I've had these tiny birds come close and chat, but no hands-on interaction … yet. While cardinals leave a red slash of color in one's memory when they take wing, the chubby little chickadees, with their endearing antics, are the birds that keep me smiling.

Isn't it true in life that the smallest things bring us the greatest emotional pleasure? Dew on the morning grass, the aria of a diminutive sparrow, a busy bee harvesting, sunlight dancing across a red bush, the fragrance after a rain….

For five years my family lived in the country with many feathered visitors. We had so much company, including surprise critters like deer, foxes, and (eek!) skunks that I started a yard journal to keep track of our entertaining guests. I still enjoy flipping through to read about our wildlife visitors.

Lists are a wonderful way to condense memorable occurrences…. Say, are you busy right now? Why don't we take a few minutes to make a list of some of the ways we've seen God's presence in our lives—little ways and big ways? It won't take long. Look, I'll start and then you take over....

1. This morning, Lord, I believe I saw Your hand in the wind as You shook the raindrops off my roof, and I glimpsed the edge of Your smile as the sun broke through the clouds. Thank You for reminding me that joy returns in the morning.

2. Yesterday I leaned down to smell my roses, and a rabbit jumped out. My heart thumped from the unexpected, scurried departure. When I first jumped back, I thought I heard someone giggle. Lord?

3. I lingered when I heard the sparrow's song and then I wondered: if I listen closely, will I hear this little one lift Your lovely name toward the heavens?

4. Lord, did You press the stars into the velvet night just for us? Thank You for leaving the lights on, 'cause sometimes I feel scared.

Bobbing in the Breezes

Daylilies are the kites of the garden, bobbing in the summer breezes with their festive faces in the sun. Daylilies come in vibrant flavors and delicious fragrances, making them a welcome addition to any yard. Usually grown in tiers, they often lean slightly forward, as if to meet the most reluctant of garden visitors with a trumpet of greeting. They also come in other shapes: stars, bowls, funnels, and Turk's caps.

"Lily" is no sissy when it comes to radical change. In fact, she's a trooper. This hearty beauty endures moves from fence line to garden wall and back again. And to show her willingness to bloom where she is planted, she faithfully reproduces, which allows the gardener every two or three years to divide the bounty and spread Lily's lovely countenance around the property.

I wish I had met Lily sooner. I could have used her stellar example. I've never been too flexible when it came to change, especially when uprooted from my home. I don't know why, but sameness equated with stability to me. When I

47

was pulled out of my comfort zone, where my roots already had searched out sustenance and settled in for the seasons ahead, I would begin to wilt.

Despite this response, I've spent a lifetime moving from one house to another. Most of the moves were in the same community; still, they were disruptive. I found it difficult to reestablish my emotional roots. Sometimes I wonder, "if I had bobbed in the breeze of change, turned my gaze to the Son, and continued to bloom and reproduce beauty, would I have had fewer unproductive seasons?"

Kneelers

God bless the soul who invented kneeling pads for gardeners. (In fact, a deluxe version exists that you can flip over with a handle, and voila, it's transformed into a stool so you can sit a spell. After an ample interlude, you can assume the kneeling position again.)

Surely the gardener who first came up with the idea was someone who had tired of using WD-40 on her kneecaps. I know after I've spent a few hours in the garden I walk differently—like all my hinges are detached.

The longer I live, the more I appreciate conveniences. No, let me restate that. The longer I live, the more I need conveniences. The rigors of life seem to have taken their toll on my body parts, which

Son Marty does triple duty in the garden with Mom.

affects my gardening. These days I have to pace myself, and sometimes I even turn a blind eye to tasks until my body suggests it's up to the job. Also, I've learned the advantage of sprinkling systems, garden tools on wheels, battery-operated shears, and, in a pinch, a hired extra pair of hands. My budget doesn't allow for a full-time gardener, but from time to time I do squeeze out enough for a part-time weeder or bulb planter when my travel schedule overrides my gardening time.

My son Marty presented his creaky-boned mother with one of those super-duper garden kneeler-stools last year. Now, when I'm done uprooting feisty weeds in one area and need to move to another part of the garden, the sides of my kneeler act as support pieces for me to push myself up, which sure beats the groaning, tipsy way I tried to rise up in the past. I'm sure more than once the neighbors wondered what kind of flowers I was sniffing as I wobbled about trying to regain my balance.

Of course, balance has been an issue for me for years. Or should I say "imbalance"? That's why I've found kneeling in the Lord's presence imperative. Bending the knee before Him positions us to focus and to hear His voice when, otherwise in our rush, we might miss it. And there, under the Holy Spirit's scrutiny, some serious weed pulling can take place. Then, when it's time to arise, He offers us His strong support. Besides, kneeling is a loving way to acknowledge the lordship of Christ in our lives, lest, as my mom used to say, we get too big for our own britches.

$\mathcal{S}$he stooped over the flowers

and talked about them

as if they were children.

Frances Hodgson

Wild, Weed-Whacking Woman

*H*ere's an important insight if you are a beginning gardener: If it's in your garden and it's flourishing, it's a weed. Trust me on this. The good news is that even a well-tended weed will eventually bloom, and I figure anything that blossoms deserves its day in the sun. Of course, I did go against that rule one day last summer....

My daughter-in-law called me to ask if I could assist her friend Chris, who had just moved into a new home. Along with the dwelling, Chris had inherited a swath of flowers that ran up and down slight inclines in the front of the house. But she couldn't tell which were flowers and which were weeds. That's where I could help. Patsy, alias Weed-Whacker Woman, to the rescue.

I'm a great believer in the older woman teaching the younger. The neat thing about that is there's always someone younger, no matter your age. Anyway, I was pleased to be enlisted for this endeavor.

I donned my jeans, garden clogs, flowered gloves, and wide-brimmed hat. Ta-da!

But when the three of us arrived at the house, I was overwhelmed at the number of plants crowded together in this extended flowerbed. None, of course, were in bloom.

(Lest my task be too easy.) I surveyed the bushy contents from different angles—standing, sitting, and kneeling—and finally announced in the voice of a seasoned gardener, "Girls, you can often identify a weed by its leaves." I then pointed to a jagged leaf and instructed them to extract all plants with that leaf. We saw a gazillion of them. OK, OK, there were probably a hundred. After a time we eradicated those pesky invaders, and since our (well, my) backs were beginning to whine, we called it a day.

When I arrived home, I passed by a flower patch, which is usually overlooked because it's off the beaten path, behind the garage. Lo and behold, I saw that we, too, had been invaded by that same jagged weed. Even though I was achy, I launched an aggressive weed campaign.

Halfway through the process my hubby came out and, in a tone of voice I didn't appreciate, asked, "What are you doing?" You know, when "what are you doing" means "are you out of your mind?"

"It's kind of obvious I'm weeding."

"Patsy, those aren't weeds, those are flowers."

I chuckled coyly. Then, in a parental tone, I said, "Listen, Les, why don't you work on your stained glass and leave me to do what I do best? These may look like flowers to you, but they are weeds."

"Want to bet? Leave the rest, and we'll see."

"Fine." I removed my gloves and headed for the bathtub.

Two weeks later the jagged-leafed weeds blossomed into spectacular, heady, hearty, black-eyed Susans. I called my daughter-in-law and confessed my mistake.

"Oh, that's OK," she quipped, "my friend's husband decided he didn't like the leafy look in the front and mowed down all the flowers." That made me feel better—sort of.

Even today, when Les and I walk by the black-eyed Susans in our yard, he still grins. And the Susans seem to nod at him in appreciation.

Patsy, the Weed-Whacker Woman—ta-duh! Emphasis on the "duh."

Lesson: Discern the weeds in your own garden before trying to uproot the weeds in your neighbor's.

A-Shedding
We Shall Go

One of my garden dreams has come true: I have a garden shed. Not a big one (4 x 6 feet), but a darling one. We hired a friend, Rick Pherson, to build it, and he chuckled throughout the building process at my excitement. "I've never seen anyone so delighted over a shed," he said more than once. I couldn't help myself. As I thought about it I realized why….

One summer, when I was a young girl, I visited my cousin Ann. Our family was just passing

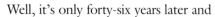

through the southern town where Ann's family lived, so we stayed only a few hours, but I would never forget that time. Much to my amazement, I found that Ann had a playhouse in her backyard. A playhouse! I thought only movie stars' children had their very own playhouses with tea sets and fussy window curtains. But here was a relative no less, just a few years older than I, with her very own space.

Well, it's only forty-six years later and

I finally have my own playhouse—masquerading as a potting shed. You won't find a tea set in the shed, but you will see my sprinkling can—the garden's teapot—perched next to my silverware (my hand tools). I didn't hang curtains, but I did have Rick hang an antique window (one hundred years old) that came out of my sister-in-law Diane's home. The window sports colored glass squares around the perimeter that look magical when the sunlight enlivens them.

Rick found two old, narrow, crackly, swing-out windows that fit perfectly with the shed's rustic décor. He covered the exterior in aromatic cedar shingles with a dapper, cedar shake roof that looks right at home nestled among the pine trees. The Dutch door creates such an inviting look when I toss open the top half.

Rick designed a workbench to fit under the front window of the shed. I added a high stool for viewing the garden, an old painted chair for friends who drop by, and oh yes, garden paraphernalia (pots, frock, gloves, seeds, hats, etc.) to make me appear legitimate. Outside stands another workbench, this one made from weathered pickets with birdhouse legs, and on the side of the shed a neighborly water pump waits patiently for someone to lay hold of its handle and give it a hearty jostle.

I have to walk through the garden to visit my potting shed, which provides me with a sense of journey as I follow the winding stepping-stones to my very own personal playhouse. Sometimes I scurry to my potting shed to take refuge from a sudden summer shower. At other times I go there to hide out from the telephone, fax, and (*shh*) pressing book deadlines. Of course I pot plants, sort seeds, and clean my tools there as well. And I confess to daydreaming about future garden possibilities in my shanty.

Where do you scurry when storms suddenly overtake you? There is One who offers to be our refuge from life's onslaught. In the safety of His presence we can dream, sort out our thoughts, and be cleansed.

Rick Pherson building my "playhouse."

Lost Path

Paths beckon us to follow them whether they meander through the woods, zigzag through a park, or circle willy-nilly around a garden. Paths speak of adventure, surprises, a way out, or a way in. The journey on a path can be fragrant or unpleasant, rocky or smooth, lonely or shared. But sometimes one can lose sight of the path.

Last summer my purple salvia were exuberant. The stunning spikes grew both tall and full, and rather than merely edging the walkway, they bulged over until the plants met right in the middle of the path. Chubby bumblebees the size of thimbles circled the blooms euphorically.

I found myself in a dilemma: should I walk the path and risk being stung, cut back the lavish growth, or detour? The path was supposed to be a shortcut to my potting shed; to go around meant I would have to take the long way.

As I contemplated my options, it occurred to me that the long way is a constant in the Scriptures when it comes to God's people. Remember the Israelites? On their journey to the Promised Land, they found themselves on a detour. In fact, they detoured for so long many of them forgot where they were going.

On the path they encountered walls of water, enemies, thirst, and death, but what really tripped them up was their reluctance and rebellion. They were reluctant to walk in

God's ways, and they expressed outright rebellion against the Almighty. Those two prickly plants will leave one's feet bleeding, so I've made a mental note to try to sidestep them.

I'm grateful the Lord offers to go ahead of us and to be our rear guard as well as our guide. He knows that the way might be perilous at times, but He will not shrink from His promises to be our path-maker. Therefore, we need not fear the path, even when it veers over an incline or winds down into the shadows of the valley.

Oh, one more thing: Sometimes the long way ends up being a divine shortcut lest we circumvent important lessons learned when lost.

So what do we do when the path before us appears impassable or is abuzz with intimidation? Follow the Lord wherever He leads, because—this is the best part—He knows the way.

gardening tips II

Nancy, Southeastern U.S.

"Ah, yes, the South, home of my birth and my life, and home of my garden. I always wonder when I'm in the garden how I can be having so much fun while working so hard! Are other jobs more delightful? I can't seem to find one!

"I feel like Oswald Chambers in overalls when I steal away for hours of digging, weeding, sweating, and planting. My heart soars to God while my feet are in the mud. How did He think of so many beautiful things, so intricately engineered, some so small, some so large, all so extravagant? *My God is an awesome God*, I think over and over again as I garden, incredulous that He would shower us with such beauty and grace.

"OK, OK, I admit it, I'm not pondering those exact thoughts while I'm breaking through tree roots to put that Francee hosta in just the right place in the shade. But later, from my kitchen window, I thank Him for giving me the strength to do what I just knew all along was right.

"And did I mention patience? I endure digging and the fertilizing and the watering during the searing heat, as I wait for my peony to mature and burst forth in miraculous beauty. No one but the Creator of the universe could have come up with this plant!

"His faithfulness endures to all generations of my Solomon's seal, my Lenten rose, and my Jacob's ladder. It never comes to an end, as year upon year, after the chill of winter, the heat of summer, the droughts and the floods, the flowers just keep coming back to grace my garden with quiet beauty.

"When I need examples of unending encouragement from my Savior and my God, I look out to see those yellow sundrops, popping up in such surprising places. How is it that He just keeps on scattering them through my life to bring such delight?

"Doesn't He ever get tired of having to lift me back up constantly, keeping my path straight, showering me with blessings, and fanning me back to life when there is only the dimly burning wick left? Evidently not. So I find myself without words to express my wonder. Here's my attempt at praise: 'From north to south to east to west, let all creation adore you, O God.'

"So, y'all can see how my little garden in the South helps me to enter into His gates with thanksgiving and His courts with praise. And just remember, girls, it's all in that soil! Make it rich with abundant amendments of humus, alfalfa, or cottonseed meal, some phosphate and a little homemade compost. Then those flowers will really have southern soul. And for the soil of the heart, let it be amended thoroughly with His precious Word so you can see Christ glorified."

Bird Brain

It started off as a Sunday afternoon stroll in the woods. I had the bright idea that Les and I should go on a bird-watching walk. We lived on property surrounded by thousands of acres of state land with many miles of trails, the perfect setting for a leisurely outing.

First we found and organized the equipment: thirty-six ounces of diet pop, two pairs of binoculars, one bird book for ID, a pen to list all sightings, and our sanguine Shih Tzu, Pumpkin.

As we headed out the door, Les asked, "Have you ever been on the trails across the road?"

By the look of the trails when we arrived, Crockett was the last one on them. The path didn't seem well defined to me, and I mentioned that to Les. He mumbled something about being a northern woodsman.

As we followed the winding path, it seemed to be closing in on us. In fact, I was thigh-high in weeds. The branches of sinister-shaped bushes and threatening trees began to smack me across the face.

"Les, get me out of here," I whined.

"You're all right. Just keep walking," he instructed, disappearing around a bend.

For a moment I was distracted from my weedy world by the sound of what I thought must be a herd of hummingbirds. It turned out to be militant mosquitoes. They motivated me to move quickly, and soon I caught up with Les. He didn't seem bothered by the mosquitoes. I think it was because of the horseflies that were devouring chunks of his hide.

My resourceful woodsman pulled off two low-hanging branches, and we took turns beating off each other's attackers.

We had been in the woods forty minutes, and I wanted to leave—now. All I had desired was to see some birds. Instead, I was branch-bruised and bug-bitten. This was no fun.

"The closest way out," Les informed me, "is the way we came in."

"No way! I'm not going back there," I stated, forging forward.

Because I had underestimated the heat, the ice cubes in the pop had long since melted. We now had Laodicean-lukewarm liquid—not very refreshing, but helpful when sloshed through the teeth to loosen the bugs from between our bicuspids. I learned that in certain circumstances it's appropriate for a woman to spit.

I was watching my feet as I moved through the thick undergrowth when something caught my eye. It was the rotting carcass of a mouse being eaten by gigantic black and yellow beetles. If I had had any lunch, I'm sure I would have lost it. I increased my pace to something close to a gallop.

We had not seen one bird. Not one!

Sweat began to drip down our branch-whipped faces, when up ahead we spotted sunlight. The woods opened up and deposited us on a dirt road at the bottom of a large hill.

As we stepped from our treacherous trail, three unsuspecting victims passed us to enter the forbidden forest. One of them had her dog on a leash. Our dog took one look at that mutt, turned around, and hightailed it right back into the thickets.

Les went running after Pumpkin, making clear reference to her intelligence and her uncertain life expectancy. A short time later he came stumbling out with a repentant pooch.

Now we had to face the hill. To say we limped up it would put us in a better light than we deserve. Les had to carry Pumpkin because she was panting so hard from her runaway escapade that we were concerned she would have cardiac arrest. I was hanging on to Les' elbow for support and motivation.

Halfway up, we sat down on the edge of the road. When we started to discuss our will, I realized this hadn't been a positive experience for us.

Finally we stumbled into our living room. As I headed for our recliner, something caught my peripheral attention. I turned and six birds were … in my front yard.

Isn't that funny? I went looking for something I already had.

Garden Patch:
Authors' Favorite Flowers and Gardens

Author	Favorite Flower	Favorite Garden
Steve Arterburn	peony	his wife Sandy's garden at their home
Jan Frank	daisy	her grandmother's
Ken Gire	gardenia	Botanic Gardens, Fort Worth, Texas
Robin Jones Gunn	gardenia, tuberose, or daffodil	the one that exists in her imagination for her yard
Liz Curtis Higgs	red tulip	her late mother's
Barbara Johnson	lilacs are #1, but everyone gives her geraniums	her own, with a white picket fence
Kevin Leman	gardenia	his cousin's garden near Bergen, Norway

Author	Favorite Flower	Favorite Garden
Florence Littauer	geranium	the Government House gardens in Auckland, New Zealand
Marilyn Meberg	long-stem, deep red roses	Tuileries Gardens in Paris or Butchart Gardens in Victoria, British Columbia
Elisa Morgan	daffodil, iris, or snapdragon	Williamsburg, Governor's Palace gardens
Francine Rivers	Joseph's coat rose or lilacs	her own
Luci Swindoll	daffodil	her friend Kurt Ratican's garden in Sebastopol, California; her own
Sheila Walsh	white tulips in a crystal vase	Monet's Garden in Giverny, France
Neil Clark Warren	*Aloe Africana*	the desert garden at The Huntington Botanical Gardens in San Marino, California
Thelma Wells	pink rose	her own organic garden with plants and herbs from the Bible

Garden Hymn

Step into my garden,
please have a seat,
here by the gate,
out of the heat.

Breathe deep my red roses
take time, dear friend.
Sip garden nectar,
escape life's din.

For here day relaxes,
flowers unfold,
and noontide streams
sunbeams of gold.

The birds feather nests,
our cares take flight,
released to float
like summer kites.

Purple infusions
brimming perfume,
drink in the fragrance
before you resume.

Walk slowly the path
that leads away,
pause to reflect
throughout your day.

For gardens God gave us
To till our heart,
To grow us strong
While we're apart.

Until the time
earth is replaced,
Eden restored
resplendent grace.

He will open the gate,
we will step in
forever day,
our Fragrant Friend.

Stepping Through
AUTUMN

Autumn's fare is color
in a leafy breeze

Frosty nights, chilly days,
cups of steamy teas.

Autumn Ambiance

*A*utumn *rocks!* I love the sweater mornings, kaleidoscope of leaves, pumpkin patches, mugs of cocoa, purple cone flowers, sweet apples, clustered sedum … Shall I continue? … Pots of mums, Indian corn, tidy asters, red burning bush, hayrides … Want more? … Bulging hydrangeas, fresh cider, golden birch, splendid pheasants, fiery maples, bristling cattails, hoards of gourds, fireplace evenings, black-eyed Susans … OK, OK, I'll stop.

I could go on and on when it comes to this invigorating season. My one complaint is that autumn isn't long enough, but then few good things are. We always want more, more,

more. We forget that once the leaves fly and the limbs lie bare, nothing is so spectacular as a snow shower that turns the trees' silhouettes into lacy, storybook pictorials.

Before the snow accumulates, leaf-raking is one of the memorable activities of autumn. As the leafy mountain grows, what child (of any age) can resist a jump smack dab in the middle of all that cushy color? Of course, leaves are a wonderful addition to the compost pile. And I also use mine to insulate some of my flower-beds for the rigors of a Michigan winter.

Don't forget to press a few leaves for the kids' school projects and for your own enjoyment. I'm quite sentimental, and I love to find old books with tiny pressed treasures between the pages.

Autumn is bulb-planting time, too, if we want a bumper crop of flowers the following spring and summer. I've learned to plant far more bulbs than I want. I'm telling you, those bulbs have a way of disappearing, thanks to Monsieur Squirrel, Captain Chipmunk, and some of their hoarding friends. But then per-haps that's their rightful due, since they were created to eat off the land, and they find it a tad inconvenient to make trips to the local supermarket for their winter sup-plies.

Actually, truth be told, I look forward to the frantic fall footwork of the squirrels as they romp purposefully about the neighbor-hood, chattering as they go. It's all part of the autumn ambiance, along with nippy air and rustling leaves.

For a complete dose of Midwest fall, add a turtleneck, a pair of jeans, a red-plaid jacket, and a trip to the apple orchard. It doesn't get any better than that. Pick up some dried flower bouquets on the way. They'll help you endure the garden-less winter ahead.

Or make your own. I love to gather hydrangeas and allow them to dry on my enclosed front porch. In late autumn I simply place them in a vase along with a few inches of water and let them slowly dry into parchment bouquets. I enjoy their antique-y appearance.

Speaking of antiques, I'm considered to be in the autumn of my life journey. I think that means I'm still colorful, but I'm beginning to lose my leaves. Come to think of it, I have noted a few leaves fluttering from my tree. For instance, I no longer skip to find the rake, my walks are shorter (hmm, is there such a thing as a walkette?), and sometimes I forget my yard chores. Oh, no, wait. I had that same malady when I was young, too.

But times do change us. Whereas once I longed to be like Martha Squirrel—busy about many things—now my desired pace would be more like Mary Scarecrow— willing to while away precious hours appreciating the beauty surrounding me. Somewhere between the squirrel and the scarecrow is a balanced pace that keeps us in the race even during the winter of our lives.

Stone Garden

My husband, Les, is so concrete. Actually, what I mean is Les enjoys gardening in concrete. He always has loved a challenge, which I'm sure is why he married cement-willed me.

Les' concrete gardening began when he set some stained glass flowers into the bottom of a mold, covered it in fast-drying diamondcrete, and an hour later unmolded his first garden stone. The result was a beautiful bouquet that promised to bloom through all seasons.

Soon my garden was sprinkled with stones in different sizes, patterns, and colors. Then visitors began to request that Les add his permanent bouquets and birds to their landscaping as well.

My favorite stone is an eighteen-inch, octagon-shaped one with a chubby rabbit right in the center. This bunny won't nibble his weight in plants. I also enjoy the one that I planted on the side of our home under a burning bush. It showcases pansies encircled in ribbons and the glass in that stone depicts deeply textured leaves on a lustrous background.

Les' stained glass iris stone is stunning as well. I placed it in a well-trafficked area so many passersby could enjoy its simple elegance.

Then Les fashioned some bricks (4" x 8") with

lettering spelling out words like "roses" and "herbs," which I found appealing and cottage-y. (I placed the rose brick next to—what else?—a rose. The herb brick I placed in front of some poppies, which has caused several folks to speculate about my cooking. No fear there—I don't do kitchens. They're way too greasy for me.)

My husband claims if you can cut out paper dolls and pour cookie batter, you can make stained-glass garden stones. It's just a matter of having the right supplies and a few basic instructions. You can make up your own designs or purchase a pattern from a stained glass supply store. They make wonderful gifts for the gardener or for the person whose only posies will be the ones on your stone.

Oh, yes, they make wonderful memory stones. My husband made a small stone to display our dog Pumpkin's name when she died a short time ago. We tucked it between some rose bushes, and every time I stop to smell the roses, I see her name and smile.

A showy cardinal with its red plumage is perched on a large stone near our entryway. It reminds me of my mother-in-law, Lena Cardinal Clairmont, who has left us for heaven's home. She continues to be missed and fondly remembered.

We leave our stones outside year-round, although I don't recommend it. Most make it through the freeze, but I did lose several smaller stones last winter. When the snows melted, I found they had turned to dust. All that was left was a handful of glass fragments.

One day I, too, am guaranteed to turn to dust—me, the fragmented one with the strong will. I'll leave this earth and head for home, where I understand the gardens are out of this world. Make room, Lena.

Roses twining toward the sky,
Woven beauty circling high.
Ivy vines interlaced,
Plaited stems wryly placed.

Covered arch in buds of pink
Sun and shadows interlink.
Sweethearts kiss in hide-a-way
Flowered veil on summer's day.

Poetry in a Vine

Oh, the cottage poetry of vines, whether they produce luscious grapes, dazzling flowers, or lush foliage. Vines invite investigation.

Vines are considered weak because they can't stand on their own, but I think of them as wise enough to reach out for help. We should be so willing in our feebleness to search for support, the kind that allows us to grow tall and strong. Besides, who knows what lingers behind a lattice of vines? Perhaps one may discover a wooden swing, a sequestered nook, a leafy library, or a friend waiting with a teacup.

Vines are a versatile addition to a garden, yard, porch, post, fence, gate, or wall. And some vines show off in every season.

In my spring garden, silver lace, a delicate flowering vine, gently tangles over the arch trellis, inviting visitors to step through. When the flowers fade, they leave behind a small, leafy covering for summer, and sometimes they then reflower in the fall to make one last, lacy statement.

Vines make lovely coverings for latticework and don't require a horticultural degree to grow. When we lived in another home in Michigan, I had a large trellis that sheltered the steps to our front porch, for which I planted a vine called the Dutchman's pipe. In the spring it produced small, white, pipe-shaped flowers (unimpressive), then throughout the summer and fall the large, heart-shaped leaves (very nice) provided cool shade on steamy days. Both the silver lace vine and Dutchman's pipe are fast growers and usually will cover your arches within the first season.

In fact, if you aren't attentive, the silver lace tendrils will vine over the trellis and then out in all directions (like a bad hair day). Once my unkempt trumpet vine held the mailman hostage for several days before we clipped him out of its clutches. A brisk trim a few times a season keeps it tidy, flowering, and under control.

I also have used morning glories, clematis, Jacob's ladder, and wisteria to dazzle a trellis, fence, or wall. All of these are showy and love a good climb. Clematis, Jacob's ladder, and wisteria are perennials and can give you years of pleasure.

Morning glories need to be planted each year, but their amazing colors and large flowers make them worth the effort. Glories close in the late afternoon and then, after a good night's rest, reopen in the morning. The blossoms, while soft hues, are either intense shades of blue (a mix of the sky and the sea), pink (the color inside a bunny's ears), or a yummy purple.

I'm enamored with clematis as well because it offers so many varieties that you can enjoy the blooms from spring through autumn. Clematis blossoms can be small or large but almost always, when clustered, are showstoppers. One season I coaxed a clematis up the side of a trellis, but its life was cut short by a (sob) weed-whacker.

I must mention one more flowering vine. This one knocks off my socks—the bougainvillea. My California visits are made even more memorable by this exciting flower. The fuchsia blossoms are especially stunning against the beige and terra-cotta world of the desert, as the plants drape down walls and climb up trellises. Bougainvillea is like a fiesta inside a flower. Olé!

A vine is worthy of being wrapped up in, whether it be from the list above or any of those twining their way around your neighborhood (grapevine, ivy, roses). If you haven't tried a vine, consider starting one up a fence post, over a cyclone fence (adds privacy and beauty), or across a barren wall. Then stand back and cheer!

Garden Glossary

Patsy Clairmont

annuals = snowbirds

bouquet = fistful of heaven

compost = my lasagna

dandelions = Mom's delight

fireflies = garden nightlights

gate = swinging sentry

hoe = no laughing matter

horticulturist = one who is willing to eat dirt on a daily basis

gardener = same as above only without the benefit of utensils

perennials = faithful companions

rabbit = fluffy felon

shovel = precedes chiropractic visits

trellis = romantic interlude

variegated = a stripe of a different color

watering can = garden teapot

weeds = main garden staple

wood chips = tree's worst nightmare

A Parade of Roses:
A Trilogy of Love Stories

LOVE'S BLOOM

The growing tension between the husband and wife as they drove home caused the silence to hang in the air like accusations. The man turned his gaze to the road and wished he were somewhere else, anywhere else, so he could escape the uneasiness of the moment. He realized he was in the wrong, but he feared a simple apology would sound trite. So he stared ahead, hoping the miles would go quickly.

His wife sat huddled in her aching emotions, wishing he would say something, anything. But even more she wished her husband could hear her heart. She loved him, and she didn't doubt his love for her. His offense was not major, but the weight of minor skirmishes had mounted up inside her, and she wanted him to care for her more tenderly—to treasure her in the presence of others and in the quiet moments alone.

Suddenly the man pulled the van to the side of the road, swung open his door, and stepped out into the night. Concerned, his wife broke the silence. "Where are you going?"

"I'll be right back." He moved out of her view.

Several moments passed, and then the van door opened. The woman looked up, and much to her amazement, her handsome husband stood there with a boyish grin, arms outstretched as he offered her a dozen long-stemmed roses sprinkled with baby's breath and wrapped in green florist tissue.

"But … but where did you get these?" She was stunned and softened by the gift.

"I saw something lying on the side of the road, and I knew I had to stop. I don't know where they came from, but would you accept them with my apology? I'm sorry."

She felt his sincerity, and his offenses dissolved in her heart.

Later that night, as they lay in each other's arms, they prayed for one another … and for the one who was so disheartened that she had thrown her lovely bouquet into the darkness.

Now, I must tell you that this is a true story, but I've left out my friends' names to protect their privacy, and besides, we who are married could all drop in our names since we each have been through moments of conflict with our mates. May we be wise enough to offer each other the flowers of kindness, thoughtfulness, tenderness, and sincerity, for they cause love to stay in full bloom.

A PROFUSION OF PETALS

*M*y friend Lana was led down a path of pain and found that, even in the darkest hours, her Savior was close enough to hear her heart break and to catch her every tear. After experiencing major losses through death and divorce, Lana found herself with no one but the Lord to turn to for comfort. That was when she learned He not only would extend comfort but also was willing to be a husband to her.

On a sunlit day, Lana decided to drag her cloudy soul outdoors and take what she hoped would be a therapeutic walk. As she strolled, she quietly talked with the Lord about her losses and her loneliness. Then she noticed, growing up a wall next to a house in her neighborhood, cloudlike clusters of pink roses. The billowing beauties stopped her in her tracks.

Then, as she walked on, she thought, *I have no one to give me roses*. Sadness began to well up in her eyes. Then she heard a whisper within her heart, "I will take care of you."

Believing it to be the Lord's voice, she whispered, "Yes, Lord, You have been ever so faithful, but in my humanness I wonder, who will give me roses?"

Several days later, a friend called her and asked if Lana would like some of the flowers she was giving away from the garden of her recently deceased aunt. Lana refused the offer, explaining that she was leaving on an extended trip. But while Lana was away, her friend sent over a gardener, who planted some of the flowers in her backyard.

Several months passed before Lana ventured to the back portion of her yard, where, much to her amazement, she discovered a mass of soft pink roses exactly like the ones she had seen growing in profusion on the day of her walk. Stunned, she heard again the whispered words of the One who loved her, "I will take care of you." Fresh tears of gratitude flowed down Lana's face at the fragrant reminder of Christ's love.

THE WEDDING GIFT

One morning Missy noticed her elderly neighbor, Mr. Ling, attempting to drag his garbage out to the curb for pickup. With her fleet twenty-six-year-old feet, she raced to his aid. The task was accomplished and she headed back to her home, but not before the old man thanked her profusely.

Missy knew that Mr. Ling's wife of more than fifty years had died recently and that the loss had devastated the aging gentleman. His stride had been broken by his fractured heart, and Missy knew how that felt. Several years earlier Missy's brother, Jeff, had died, and the loss had created a deep well of compassion within her for others who struggled with ongoing sadness.

From time to time Missy assisted her neighbor with other small tasks, and they developed a warm regard for each other's well-being. One time Mr. Ling invited Missy to come in and see displayed on the wall pictures of his wife, children, and grandchildren. Missy noted as she left that day that her friend looked increasingly frail.

Mr. Ling had grown beautiful roses in his front yard, but after his wife's death and with his declining health, his lovely flowers began to fade from neglect. By midsummer, the bushes were leggy and budless.

One day, when Missy spotted Mr. Ling checking his mailbox, she waved and walked over to share some good news. She was engaged and planned to marry in a few months.

"Then I shall give you a wonderful gift for your special day," Mr. Ling exclaimed. He seemed pleased for an excuse to repay Missy for her many kindnesses.

But before her autumn wedding day arrived, Mr. Ling died. Missy felt disheartened in the weeks that followed when she walked out her front door and realized her dear neighbor was gone. His home looked so empty and bleak.

On Missy's wedding day, as she busily prepared for the whirlwind of activity, she glanced out the window, anticipating the bridal party's arrival. Mr. Ling's home was still sitting vacant, but Missy's attention focused on something in the front yard she hadn't seen before.

She made her way out the front door and across the street. There, in Mr. Ling's yard, was one white rose in full bloom. Missy's heart skipped a beat as she recalled her friend's words, "And I shall give you a wonderful gift for your special day." Missy drew the flower to herself and whispered, "Oh, Mr. Ling, it is a wonderful gift. Thank you."

Garden Artist

*A*re you an artist? No, let me restate that. You *are* an artist! Now, I know some of you are groaning and insisting that you are three colors short of a palette.

Yes, I, too, protested loudly about my un-artsy ways and even followed my protest up with what I felt was undeniable proof: several floral watercolors that were—ahem—less than the best. But I've since learned not to be so harsh about my efforts or others' because art is all about risk, perspective, and growth. Yes, gifted artists do exist—the Georgia O'Keefes, Bessie Pease Gutmans, and Monets of this world. But there are also the Grandma Moseses (late bloomers) and the Ethel Hockenshocks (sketching at her kitchen table in Hackensack), and the Patsy Clairmonts (scribbling on the backs of envelopes).

Patsy Clairmont

Today I realize that art takes many forms: the arranging of flowers in a vase, the placement of lawn ornaments, the design of a vegetable bed, the photograph of a morning as it awakens the garden. I do love it that God has set the standard by being such a freewheeling artist. Why, He puts colors together that decorators say don't match, and creates breathtaking art out of it. He gives us the same liberty to break the art rules.

As of late I've been tinkering with a new camera and have been delighted with some of the resulting photographs. I mean, who can go wrong with models that strike the pose of a willowy iris, a pudgy lilac, or a cluster of black-eyed Susans? When I finish a roll of film, I can hardly wait to see the prints. Though they aren't all prizewinners, if I capture even one frame in fifty that's dappled in sun and shadow in a way that dazzles the eye, I'm exhilarated. I run around making every passerby look at the result of my efforts to capture His handiwork. I can't imagine how thrilled God must have been with His originals.

We're all artists in different areas and to varying degrees. Even though I'll never win acclaim for my photography,
I find in it personal satisfaction and pleasure. It's my recess, a place for my emotions to find creative expression (which really wins over, say, griping).

We were created after the Greatest Artisan of them all; so let's dip into the untapped reservoirs of our giftedness and explore the artist in ourselves!

The world is charged
with the grandeur of God.

GERARD MANLEY HOPKINS

gardening tips III

Florence, the Midwest

"Of all the hobbies I've had in my eighty-six years, I do believe flower gardening is at the top of the list. I wouldn't trade my early mornings in the yard, watching nature come alive in spring, for anything I've ever experienced—next to childbirth, that is. You know you're hooked when an old friend calls just as you are going out the door in your gardening togs and asks if you would like to meet her for lunch, but you decline.

"Now me, I want to respond with, 'I'd rather eat dirt,' but nice old ladies are expected to have good excuses for everything, so I say something like, 'My roses are in trouble, and I must attend to them today. Let's go to lunch tomorrow; I hear it will be raining.' There are enough rainy days in our lives to do that other stuff, don't you think?"

Things I've Learned the Hard Way

1. Unlike vegetable gardening, in which everything grows in rows for easier cultivating, flowers look best in bunches or singles, depending on the plant's size.

2. Start small and add plants only when you decide how much time you want to spend on your hobby. You can find yourself with more chores than time to finish them—I know. After all, flower gardening is meant to be fun.

3. In the fall, prepare plots for spring planting. And think where you would like to see some early flowers like tulips, daffodils, and grape hyacinth, all of which should be planted in the fall. What a thrill to look forward to seeing what pops up from those six-inch holes you dug last fall!

4. Spring is the time to treat yourself to lots of trips to your local nurseries. But you'll need self-control. Remember, the plants often are ready before you are. Don't buy until you can go right home and plant, and even then buy only one thing at a time. The temptation to indulge can be overwhelming, but remember, keep it small.

5. I think every garden should have daylilies. They are so beautiful and multiply every year.

Fall's Fireworks

Trees and autumn are almost synonymous in my part of the country, for with the loss of summer flowers, midwestern trees fill the land with year-end color. The brilliant foliage keeps our landscape exciting and even, at certain bends in the road, magnificent.

My mom always felt trees made property more valuable and beautiful. Don't tell my mom, but I'm of the opinion that some trees are nothing but t-r-o-u-b-l-e. I know; I've owned a few. They are what I affectionately refer to as "trash trees." You know, the ones that produce ugly stuff that looks like cigar debris or tobacco wads. These unsightly castoffs from the tree are tossed around by the winds, leaving an ugly path throughout the neighborhood that causes neighbors' lips to purse when they pass you, the owner of the tree, in the grocery store.

And what about the trees whose roots are like tentacles, looking to choke out the life of your septic system, part your driveway like the Red Sea, or disembowel your sidewalk? One year I planted some bamboo trees for a privacy screen next to our deck. What I didn't realize was that bamboo has a sneaky habit of sending out leader trees underground that pop up in neighbors' yards. Those are the same neighbors who didn't desire a privacy screen, a bamboo tree, a koala bear, or now us as neighbors.

Many trees produce lovely flowers, fruit, and fall color without the negative fallout. Of course, before planting a fruit tree, one should realize they are labor intensive because of the pruning, the fruit felons that attack the tree, and the autumn debris. Yet I think a few fruit trees are worth the seasonal struggles.

Yes, trees offer many rewards: sipping iced tea under the shade of a wonderful tree; tying a swing to a high branch and trying to touch the clouds with your toes; or taking a nap in a hammock stretched between two tree trunks. And I surely wouldn't want to miss out on the flaming red and yellow maples in the autumn. They are fall's fireworks.

Trees add stability, beauty, and value, which is probably why Scripture encourages us to become like well-watered trees, trees that are lush with foliage, deep in roots, and continually bear fruit (see Psalm 1:3; Jeremiah 17:8).

Branch out in your life by spending time in the Scriptures. Turn to the concordance in the back of your Bible and look up all the verses listed under "tree" and "fruit." I think you'll be encouraged and instructed … I was.

Some of my favorite trees:

Saucer Magnolia

The short-lived, stupendous flowers are followed by delightful, oval-shaped, mint-colored leaves that deepen for autumn interest.

Top: Japanese Maple
Bottom: Dogwood

Japanese Maple

This tree is a miniature way to add a little frill and a lot of color-depth to your garden.

Bartlett Pear

The fruitless version of this tree has beautiful flowers in the spring and colored leaves in the fall.

Apple

The gnarly trunk and limbs add a sense of history to the landscape.

Flowering Plum

This plum-pretty tree develops dark leaves and in spring, dainty flowers.

Dogwood

Bark up this tree and find lovely pink or white spring flowers looking back atcha.

Weeping Cherry

Cheers me up somehow.

Blue Spruce

A great refuge for birds,
this tidy tree lends gentle coloration
and a wonderful shape to the garden.

Birch

Has a great parchment look.

Crab Apple

Well, it just fits my personality.

Palm Tree

Pass me a coconut, dah-ling.
On windy days, palms look like
feather dusters sweeping the sky.

Crab Apple

Stepping Through
WINTER

*W*inter's icy breath
Against window panes

Wonderland of white
Upon garden lanes.

The Winter Ball

A fresh snowfall crochets a garden into a fairy tale. Even though one may not be able to gather a frosty bouquet to take indoors, it certainly turns the barren outdoors into a wonderland of icicles, snow mounds, drifts, and dreams. My garden ornaments are transformed into princesses garbed in white fur as they await their carriage for the winter ball. Frozen prisms fastened tight to my windows scatter sunlight in crystal shafts across the ledges. Under the icy spell, garden stakes become magic wands, piles of brush become cushioned tufts, and the trellis a lacy grand entrance for the queen. Come one! Come all! It's winter!

When the winter cold hangs on too long (brrr), as it most always does (regardless how beautiful), it builds a growing anticipation in my heart for spring buds. Then I have to remind my impatient heart that the land needs the long rest if it's to flourish again. Not unlike us.

I personally find it difficult to rest, even though I must admit, once you finally coax me into a chair, I certainly can sit deep. It's wheedling me into the chair that's the challenge. I always have so much to do, or at least that's how I look at the world. And now that I'm in the autumn of my life, I feel a greater urgency to be productive before winter permanently sets in.

Yet I find my best efforts thin out fast without the benefit of restorative sleep. Sometimes I just need to climb into my igloo, pull a snowy-white blanket over me, and drift off. Otherwise I run about two quarts shy of enough antifreeze, leaving me at best sluggish or, at the worst, stalled in some snow bank. And take my word for it, a snow bank isn't a good place to cash in on life.

Better yet, take the Lord's Word for it. He's far more reliable and extends an irresistible invitation to us all, "Come to me ... and you will find rest for your souls" (Matthew 11:28-29). He knows that we, like the land, need to rest if we are to blossom again. So, if you're in a winter season, with the biting winds of adversity nipping at your heels, or if you're just plain tuckered out from life's flurry, take a break, my friend.... You'll need your rest for the ball.

One night came Winter
noiselessly and leaned
Against my
window-pane.

CHARLES G.D. ROBERTS,
"THE FROSTED PANE"

You Can't Do That

Just prior to Christmas one year a friend sent me an amaryllis bulb, pot, directions, and even a bag of special soil. I was elated but far too busy to plant the flower. Now, folks, when we are too busy to plunk one bulb into prepared soil, we are way too busy. Nonetheless that was my dilemma. I was thankful to note the directions said that, if I wanted to wait awhile before planting (they must have seen my calendar), I should store the bulb in a dry, dark place.

So I slid my gift into the recesses of my kitchen pantry and went about my schedule, which included a ten-day speaking trip. When I returned, I immediately jumped into unearthing and distributing throughout the house our holiday decorations. I was hanging tinsel when I remembered my bulb and decided after I completed the project at hand I would fish out the directions and finally plant my present.

Do you like surprise presents? I do. And did I get one when I opened the pantry door. A three-stemmed, gloriously blooming amaryllis greeted me. Its stalks—yes, stalks—ranged from twelve to seventeen inches high. I mean, we're talking future Jack-in-the-beanstalk material.

I was dumbfounded. I looked at the plant, the sealed bag of soil, the dark abode of the pantry, and announced, "You can't do this! You haven't been planted yet. You haven't been watered. You don't have any soil. You don't have any light except for faint flickers through the louvers. How can this be?"

I pulled out the pot, opened the bag of soil, dumped it into the pot, and hastily patted it around the thriving bulb. (As if, at this point, it needed my assistance.)

I've often been filled with the same kind of wonder as I've met women who have gone through years of hardships and losses. I've wondered how they survived dark years of existence, often without what we feel are the basic necessities of life. They've made it without an environment of nurturing soil, without the water of human compassion, and with only flickers of light. Yet they lived—even grew and, yes, blossomed. How can this be?

I have a new friend who is acquainted personally with extreme loss. She was taken from her home as a toddler and placed in a sanitarium for those with tuberculosis, where she lived for years. Rarely did she see her mother, and often the hospital staff, busy with their unending chores, had little time left for nurturing a child. Yet somehow, through the dark recesses of her life, she leaned toward the faint flickers of light offered sporadically by the kind intentions of the nursing staff, and today she has blossomed into a gentle-hearted, wise, discerning woman.

I'm dumbfounded; often that which has had to grow in the dark can be both exquisite and fragrant. And that thought casts a new light on suffering.

Winter's Grip

Winter's grip
icy
upon
Autumn's leafy
shoulder.

Day shivers
into
night
Dreaming of
spring's dawn.

Deck the Halls

The world depends on flowers. Really it does—far more than we might realize. Take, for instance, weddings. They require blossoms even if it's only a simple bouquet or a single bud. I ask you, how could one become a bride without flowers? I personally carried an orchid with ribbon streamers atop a small white Bible. Later the orchid detached and became a corsage that I wore on my going away suit. Spiffy, huh?

It isn't only weddings that are immersed in flowers. What about funerals? We find a touch of solace even in the midst of our grief as beautiful arrangements arrive. The fragrances gently remind us that seasons change, spring will return, and that people truly care about our loss.

Can you imagine the Rose Parade without roses? How about Easter without lilies? Or Mother's Day without a spring (daisy, daffodil, or tulip) arrangement. Or Thanksgiving minus gourds, pumpkins, Indian corn, yellow- and rust-colored mums. Guests coming? Better pick some flowers for the table and their room. (I stayed recently at my friend Andrea's home. She had it festooned with flowers: lilacs, tulips, roses, and ranunculus. The petaled ambiance was dreamy, and the perfume of that memory still lingers in my mind.) Do you need to acknowledge someone's special day, accomplishment, anniversary, new home, or baby? How about wiring carnations and candy? Flowers spruce up some of our most important occasions as nothing else can do.

No, don't worry, I didn't forget Christmas, I was saving it. It's such a festive package to unwrap, for the holy holiday season abounds in flowers, greenery, and plants. Christmas cactus, evergreen boughs, sprigs of holly, balls of mistletoe, and endless pots of poinsettias. We find even this frosty season blossoming in floral tradition.

In fact, I personally like to fill the winter season with blooms. I find it helps cheer the hours as sunlight wanes to have not only a bud vase on my nightstand but also bed sheets that burst in garden fare. I add flowers via fabrics, rugs, and pillows. One of my favorite places to watch the winter fire sizzle is in an oversized, soft-cushioned, yellow-flowered chair that resembles a chintz teacup. What fun to sit deep and steep in dreams of spring's return.

Speaking of teacups, I am drawn to floral- and fruit-covered dishes that bring the garden indoors in a most delicious way. Last holiday season Les and I decided on a new, bold, and beautiful dish set that features birds, ribbons, and evergreen. A real plus to us was that the artist lives in our community. The black-capped chickadees, cardinals, and other garden birds keep our table conversations chirping (and remind us to fill our outdoor feeders).

Another way I stave off the winter doldrums is to leaf through old and new garden magazines, as well as seed catalogs, which help me plan for spring planting.

Yes, flowers have a way of blooming all year long.

Hummers

We were wintering in the desert, when early one morning Les stepped into the condo with his hands cupped. He nodded in my direction, and I stepped closer to see what treasure he had found. He carefully opened his hands, and there, under the gentle pressure of his thumb, was a velvet, iridescent hummingbird. Seems the tiny wonder had flown up inside our unfurled patio umbrella and then couldn't find the exit. We decided he was a new, inexperienced flier whose compass went bonkers when he suddenly was surrounded by spokes and canvas. Before Les set the captive free, he couldn't resist first sharing the little fellow with me. After I oohed appropriately three times in succession, Les stepped to the door and released the flyer back into the morning.

These petite acrobats surround our condo, entertaining us with their aerodynamics. Their frenetic air shows across our patio position us in the direct line of flight, which evidently irritates them. They will flit right up to our faces as if to say, "Who do you think you are?" Hovering inches away from our noses, they let it be known that they are neither intimidated nor deterred by our presence.

To accommodate them, Les maintains an elongated red feeder filled with sweet water for their enjoyment. By the number of times each day they visit, I'd say their joy is plumb full and splashing over.

One day, as I sat on the patio drinking a

milk shake out of a paper cup decorated with red lettering, a hummingbird swooped past my eyes and hung as though suspended by invisible threads in front of my cup while he attempted to draw nectar out of the red print. Then, as if I had purposely pulled a prank on him, he dashed up to my face, looked me over from forehead to chin several times, and then, disgusted (I could see it in his little eyes), darted away. Well!

My husband's involvement with these pee-wee tricksters is actually quite amiable. In fact, he frequently offers them free showers under the arced spray from the garden hose, and they often take him up on it. Flitting back and forth, allowing the water droplets to illuminate their iridescent bodies, the hummingbirds seem to appreciate his efforts, or maybe they appreciate that the showers are free. Anyway, it appears mutually satisfying.

Speaking of satisfying, one morning Les greeted me with, "Hey, you missed the excitement, Patsy."

"Really? What happened?"

"A female hummingbird flew into the window and knocked herself silly. I retrieved her from the bushes and held her in my hands until the shock wore off, and then she darted away," he reported with enthusiasm.

"Wow!" I exclaimed, impressed with his avian endeavor. Then, puzzled, I asked, "Was she wearing her tutu? How did you know it was a female?"

This is when, like morning sun on a meadow, the satisfied look began to spread across his face. "By her driving, of course."

Les, the quipster

gardening tips IV

Kellie Frank, Southern California

1. Some plants to start with:

Tomatoes	Carrots	Impatiens
Lettuce	Broccoli	Pansies
Cauliflower	Any bulbs	Poppies

    You can see growth in all these plants daily, so they encourage young gardeners.

2. Keep at it! The fruits of your labor will appear soon enough.

3. Although manure is gross and smells, plants love it. So, if you want beautiful plants, use it!

4. Preparing the soil is probably the least fun part of gardening (well, along with weeding), but good preparation means healthy plants.

5. The best part of gardening is that you actually get to see and eat the results.

Kellie when she started gardening at age 12. (She is now 16.)

Bouquet Blues

The day was sunny outside, but I was experiencing a petite case of the blues inside. An inexplicable swing whose triggering event I couldn't pinpoint, my mood settled in like an unwanted guest with luggage. I wasn't incapacitated by it, just aggravated because the feelings slowed down my pace, and I had much to do.

Then my dear husband walked in the door with a florist's vase of irises and transformed my day. How could a few petals redirect my feelings? I don't know. I just know they did. Perhaps their representation of the Creator's flowering touch on the hard earth reminds me of what He can do with our hard challenges, if not our hard hearts and heads (speaking for myself, of course). I'm not suggesting a fistful of posies will cure all our melancholy, but I have noted many times when a bouquet brought fresh rays of hope to an otherwise dismal outlook.

When I gather a basket of flowers, I feel as though I'm scooping up colorful specks of God's glory. When those flowers are arranged throughout the house, I think of myself spreading the glory into dim corners, brightening each space with the flowers' petaled presence. And I enjoy the varied flowered scents that waft through the air, transporting my mind to springtime even in the midst of a blizzard.

I remember staying at a hotel for a conference with demands as constant as the whipping winds of a blizzard, and I was running around like a chicken with my head cut off (as my Southern momma would say). I dashed from the conference to my hotel to change clothes and was stunned to find that an abundant bouquet of wildflowers had been delivered to my room.

What a day-brightener! The profusion of garden color was a welcome moderator for my frenetic pace. The attached note was from a publisher, wishing me a pleasant stay. I was delighted because the flowers were beautiful, yet I was perplexed because no vase accompanied this wonderful arrangement. (Did the gift-givers think I travel with a vase?) Not certain how to remedy this and needing to press on to my next responsibility, I filled one of the sinks in the bathroom, carefully laid the tissue-wrapped flowers so the lower stems were covered with water, and then hurried on my way. I thought perhaps when the maid cleaned the room she would see my need for a container and take care of it so my bouquet wouldn't die.

Later, when I returned, my flowers were still in the sink (so much for the maid). I drained out the old water and refilled the sink. Gratefully, the flowers didn't look as if they had suffered. Oh, a couple of blossoms were beginning to droop, but for the most part they continued to fill the room with beauty.

The next morning, after giving the flowers another fresh sinkful of water, I was brushing my teeth when my nose started to itch. I called to my husband, "I think some of these wildflowers are triggering my allergies. We may have to move them out of the bathroom. I really need a vase."

As I continued with my primping, my hand bumped the edge of the flowers. Something about that physical encounter caught my attention. I stopped, grabbed my spectacles, did a careful inspection of my bouquet, and laughed. They were silk. Every cotton-pickin' one of 'em. I had watered this artificial bouquet for two days and even had had an allergic response. What a hoot! No wonder the florist didn't provide a vase. No wonder the maid ignored the flowers. She must have wondered about my sanity (she's not the only one).

Today that bouquet adorns a corner in my living room and serves as a lovely reminder that life is not always what it seems, nor are my assessments (not to mention my allergies). How deflating.

Hmm, I think I feel a teensy case of the blues coming on.

120

Winter Tree

Ladyfingers dressed in lacy gloves

of new snow,

how white and feminine

you stand silhouetted against the December sky.

And, oh, there within your hair

you've tucked a finch or two.

How wise to keep a song so near.

Winds whip at your fragile form.

You shudder, nod, and curtsy.

Lady that you are, you bow but do not break.

Delicate, enduring beauty

fastened strong in rooted courage.

For Every Season
All Things He Does Well

May He who holds the sparrow
In the palm of His hand
And causes flowers to blossom
Across the desert sand

May He who lights the heavens
And sets the stars in place
Guide you through the valley
And reveal to you His face.

May the Lord who gathers storm clouds
And fills them with rain
To water earth's parched soil
That the land might give forth grain

May He move upon your heart
In the midst of life's distress
In such a way that you might know
The kindness of His press.

For He who formed the mountains
And carved out the sea
Is He who has promised
To shelter you and me.

His wings are extended
That we might draw near
To hear His constant heartbeat
And calm our every fear.

Our Alpha and Omega
Our Refuge, Our Friend
The One who holds the wind at bay
Whose days will never end

His plan is eternal
Not hampered by this life
He is our Holy Groom
And we shall be His wife.

Then finally we will know
The wonders of life's haze
As *I AM* reveals to us
The mystery of His ways

So rest in God's comfort
And be assured, dear one
He who does all things well
Will complete what He's begun.